This Is a Let's-Read-and-Find-Out Science Book™

Volcanoes

by Franklyn M. Branley
illustrated by Marc Simont

Thomas Y. Crowell New York

Other Recent Let's-Read-and-Find-Out Science Books™ You Will Enjoy

Flash, Crash, Rumble, and Roll · What Happens to a Hamburger · Dinosaurs Are Different · Volcanoes · Germs Make Me Sick! · Meet the Computer · How to Talk to Your Computer · Rock Collecting · Is There Life in Outer Space? · Comets · All Kinds of Feet · Rain and Hail · Why I Cough, Sneeze, Shiver, Hiccup, & Yawn · You Can't Make a Move Without Your Muscles · The Sky Is Full of Stars · The Planets in Our Solar System · Digging Up Dinosaurs · No Measles, No Mumps for Me · When Birds Change Their Feathers · Birds Are Flying · A Jellyfish Is Not a Fish · Cactus in the Desert · Me and My Family Tree · Redwoods Are the Tallest Trees in the World · Shells Are Skeletons · Caves · Wild and Woolly Mammoths · The March of the Lemmings · Corals · Energy from the Sun · Corn Is Maize

The *Let's-Read-and-Find-Out Science Book* series was originated by Dr. Franklyn M. Branley, Astronomer Emeritus and former Chairman of The American Museum-Hayden Planetarium, and was formerly co-edited by him and Dr. Roma Gans, Professor Emeritus of Childhood Education, Teachers College, Columbia University. For a complete catalog of Let's-Read-and-Find-Out Science Books, write to Thomas Y. Crowell Junior Books, 10 East 53rd Street, New York, NY 10022.

Printed in the United States of America. For information address Thomas Y. Crowell Junior Books, 10 East 53rd Street, New York, N.Y. 10022. Published simultaneously in Canada by Fitzhenry & Whiteside Limited, Toronto.
10 9 8 7 6 5 4 3 2 1
First Edition

Library of Congress Cataloging in Publication Data
Branley, Franklyn Mansfield, 1915–
Volcanoes.

(Let's-read-and-find-out science book)
Summary: Explains how volcanoes are formed and how they affect the earth when they erupt.
1. Volcanoes—Juvenile literature. [1. Volcanoes]
I. Simont, Marc, ill. II. Title. III. Series.
QE 521.3.B73 1985 551.2'1 84-45344
ISBN 0-690-04451-8
ISBN 0-690-04431-3 (lib. bdg.)

In the year 79 Mount Vesuvius, a volcano in Italy, blew up.

Hot, melted rock from deep inside the earth pushed up through the mountain. The top of the mountain exploded. Ash, cinders and stones buried Pompeii, a great city below the mountain.

Nearly two thousand years later Mount Vesuvius still spouts steam and ash. But not as much as it did long ago.

In 1815 the same thing happened in Indonesia, a group of islands between Asia and Australia. Mount Tambora blew its top. Billions of tons of the mountain were turned into ash. They were thrown into the air.

Winds carried the ashes all around the earth. They made a cloud that blocked out the sun. The earth got colder and colder.

The next year, 1816, was called the year without a summer. The New England states had 6 inches of snow in June, and there were frosts in July and August. That's how cold it was.

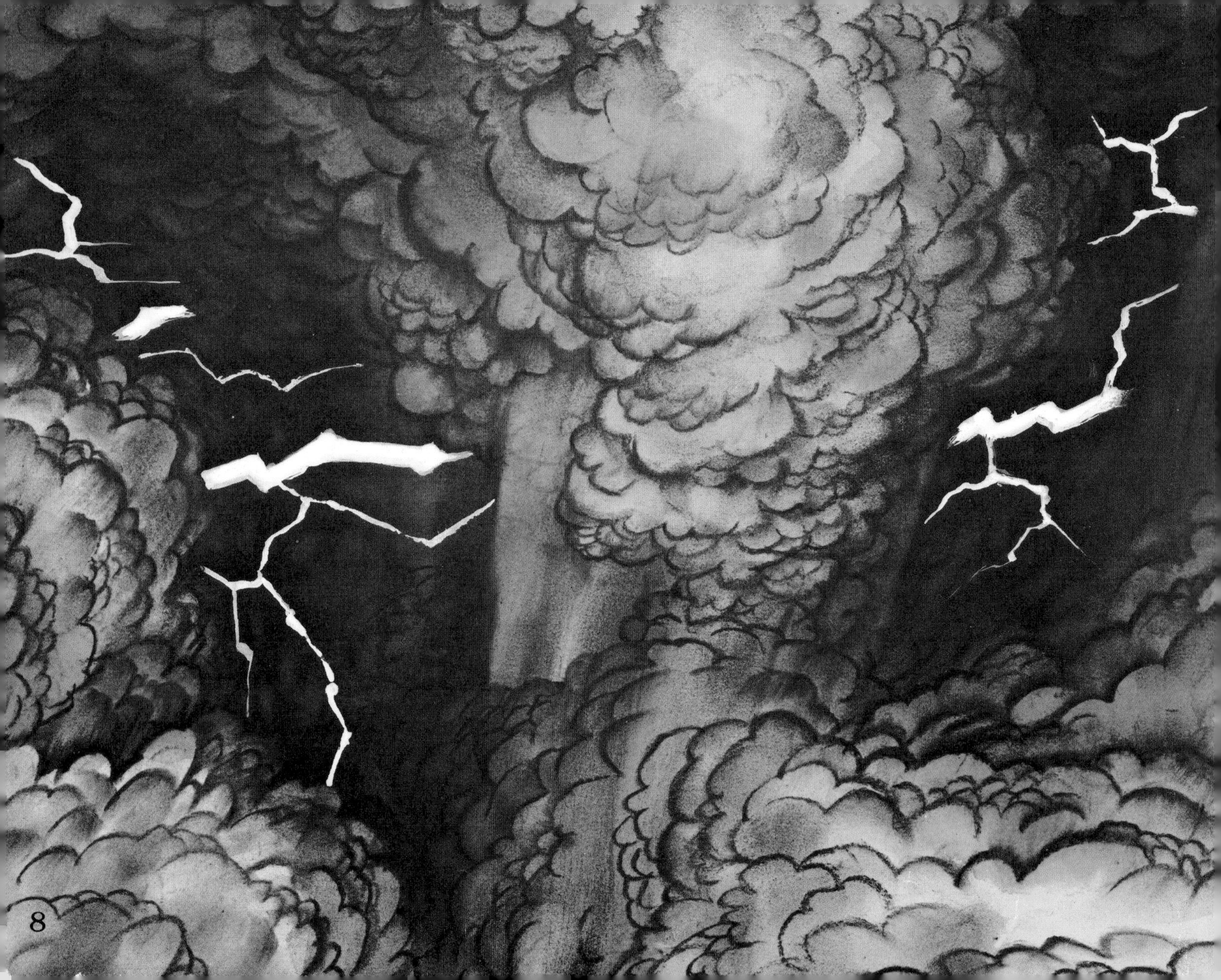

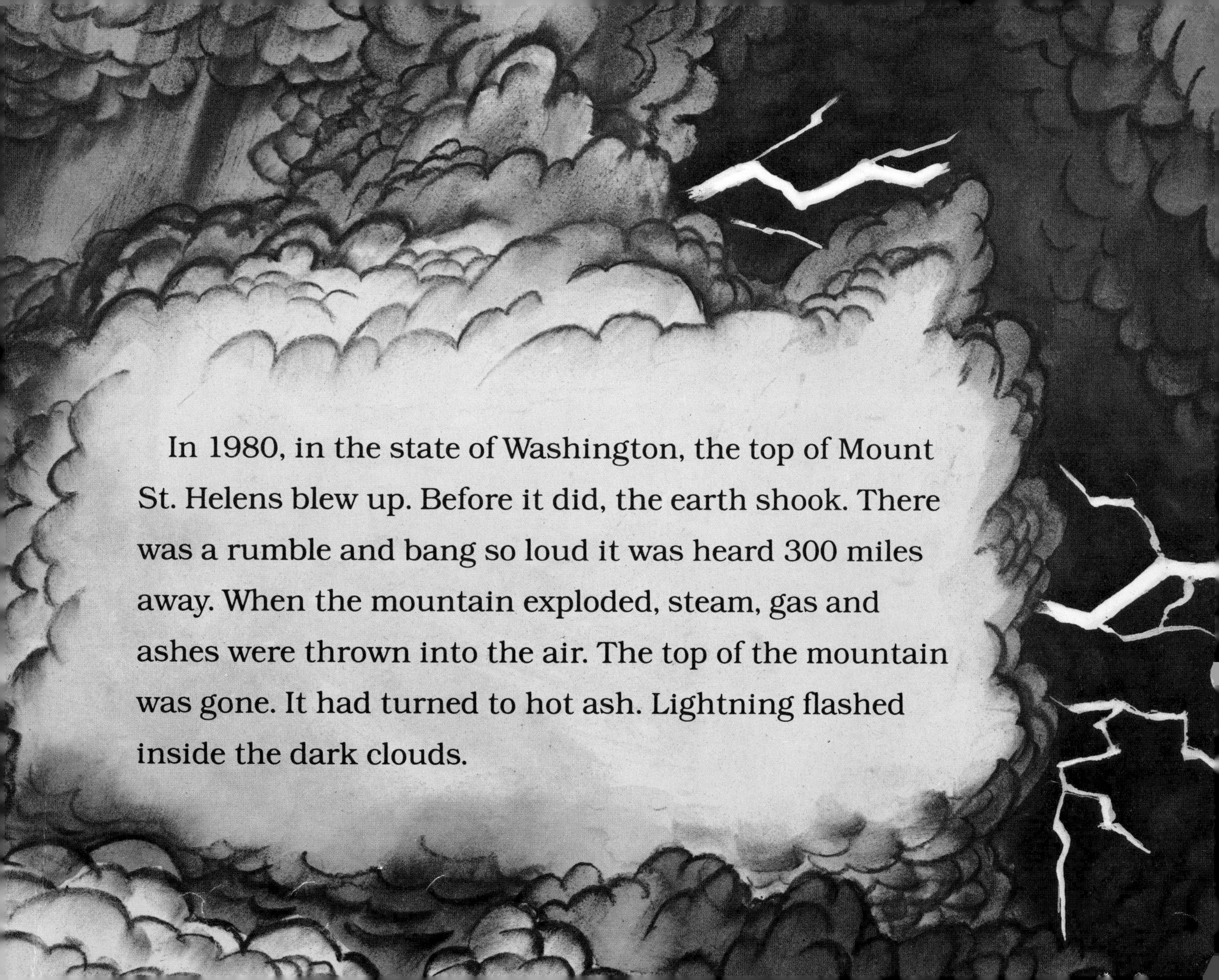

In 1980, in the state of Washington, the top of Mount St. Helens blew up. Before it did, the earth shook. There was a rumble and bang so loud it was heard 300 miles away. When the mountain exploded, steam, gas and ashes were thrown into the air. The top of the mountain was gone. It had turned to hot ash. Lightning flashed inside the dark clouds.

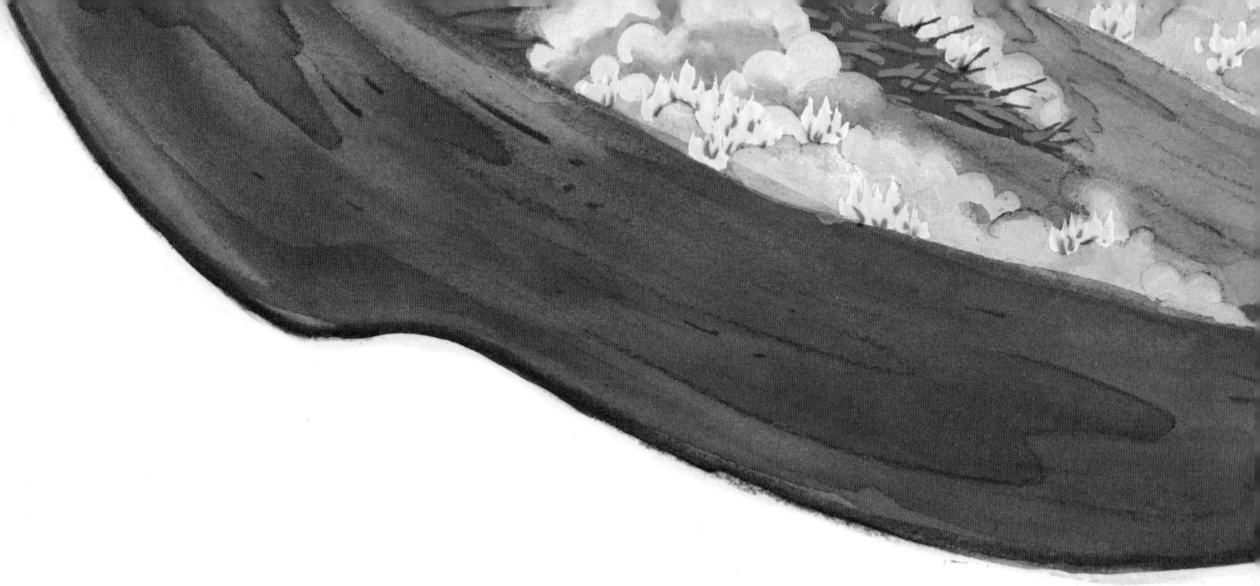

Huge trees were flattened by the blast. Here and there the heat started fires. The hot ash melted snow on the mountain and made a thick mud that flowed down the sides. The mud covered fields and forests. Lakes, ponds and rivers were filled with it. The mud buried animals, houses and people.

The eruption of Mount St. Helens was not a surprise. Geologists, people who study the earth, knew that the volcano had erupted about 100 years ago. And it was bound to happen again.

Geologists watch volcanoes for signs of an eruption. They listen for rumblings. Mount St. Helens had been rumbling off and on for more than a hundred years. Geologists knew that these rumblings were warnings.

Geologists also measure earthquakes. Before a volcano erupts, there are usually earthquakes in the region.

Volcanoes and earthquakes occur because our planet is always changing. Parts of it are always moving.

The earth is covered with soil, sand and broken rocks. Under that are layers of solid rock called the crust. The crust is broken into huge sections called plates. Geologists have given the plates names.

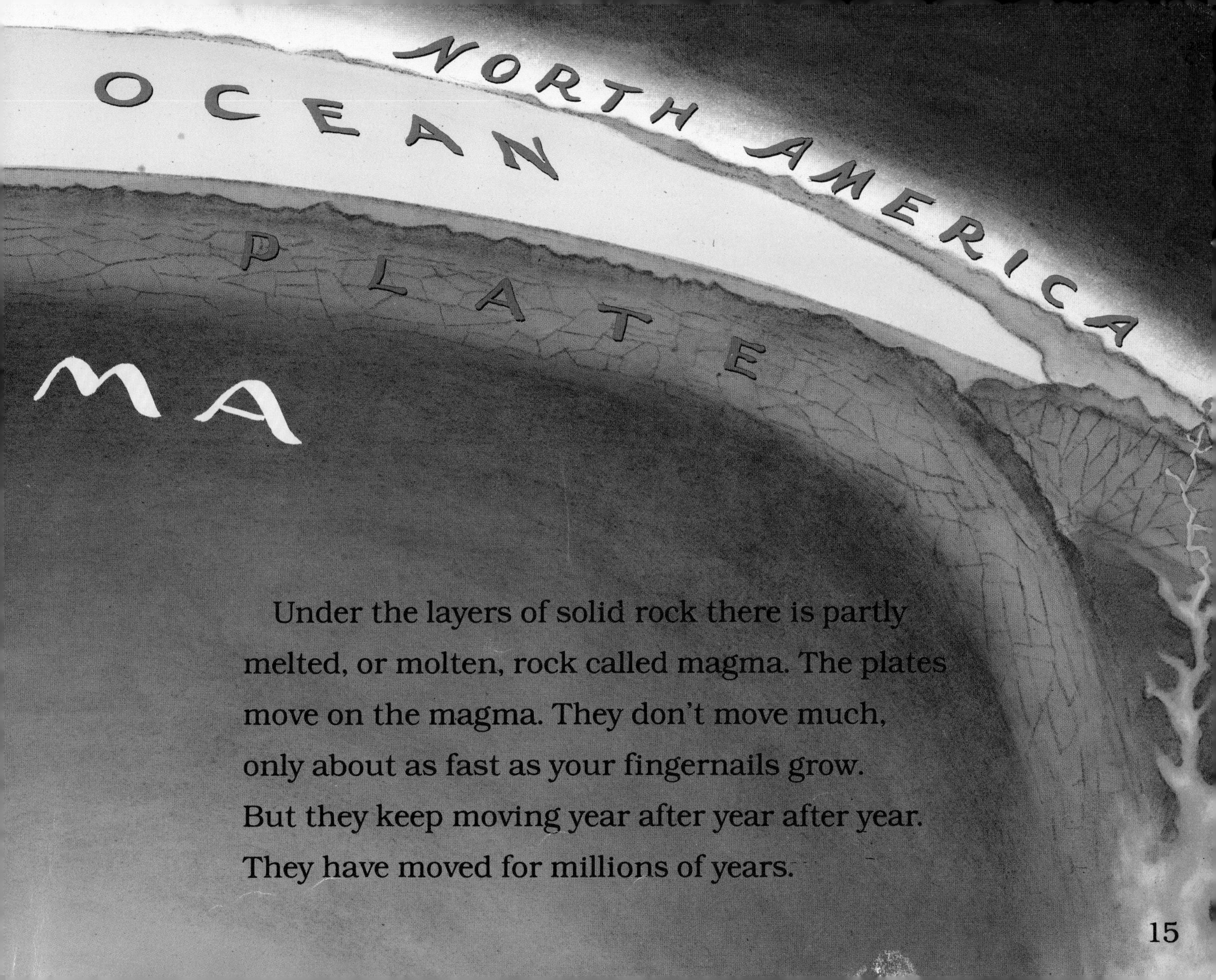

Under the layers of solid rock there is partly melted, or molten, rock called magma. The plates move on the magma. They don't move much, only about as fast as your fingernails grow. But they keep moving year after year after year. They have moved for millions of years.

In some places two plates move apart. Where they do, hot magma pushes up between them. After it comes to the surface, magma is called lava. The lava cools and becomes solid rock. That is happening in places under the oceans right now. Huge underwater mountain ranges have been building up for millions of years.

In some places plates move apart. In other places they push together and one plate moves under another. Or one plate may slide past another.

These movements shake the earth. They make earthquakes.

At Mount St. Helens an edge of the small Juan de Fuca Plate has been moving under the North American Plate for thousands of years. As it has moved under, the heavy plates have rubbed together. The friction between the plates made the lower plate hot enough to melt. The hot, molten rock pushed upward. Most of the magma stayed under the mountain. It pushed upward but did not break through. Some came through cracks in the side of Mount St. Helens.

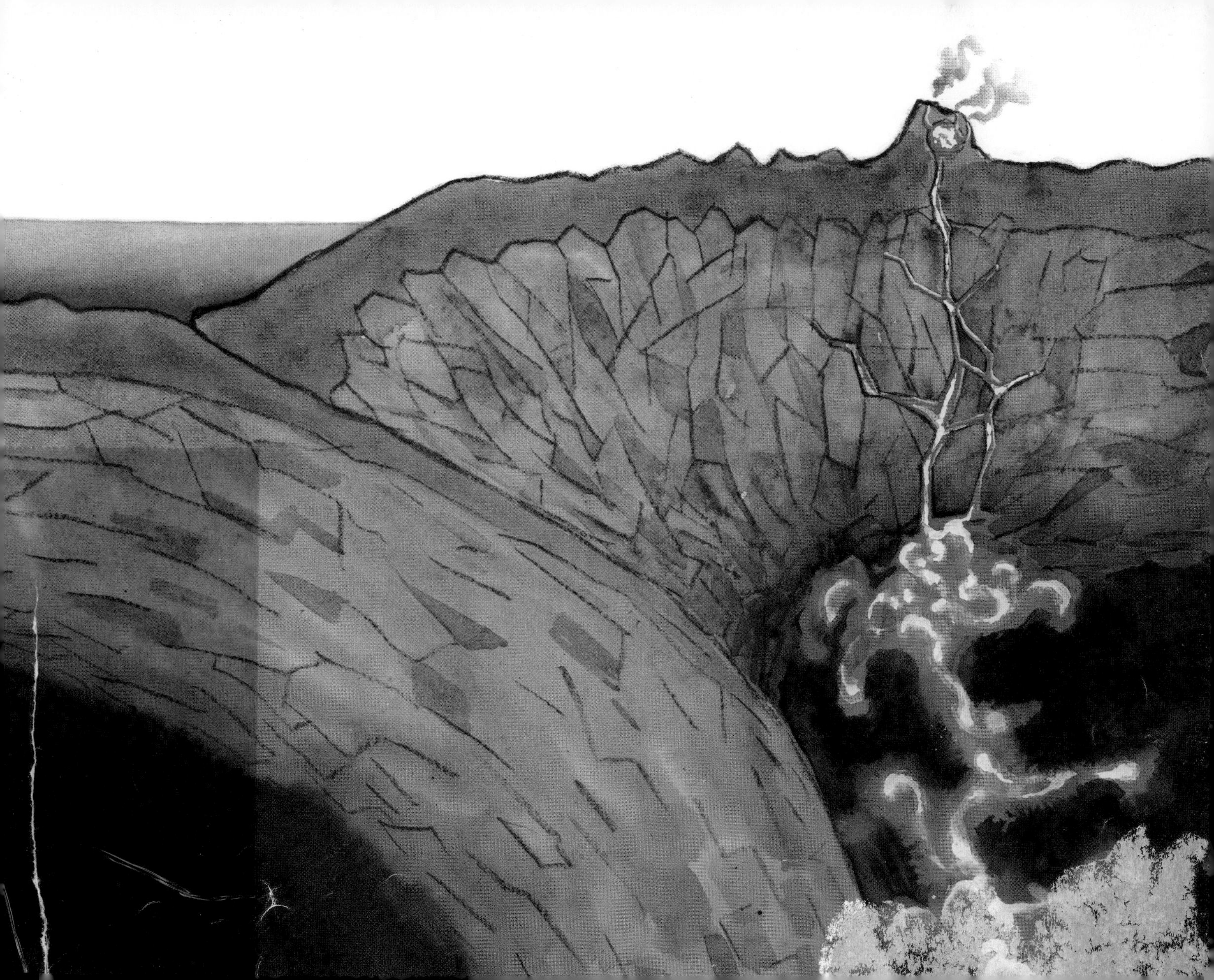

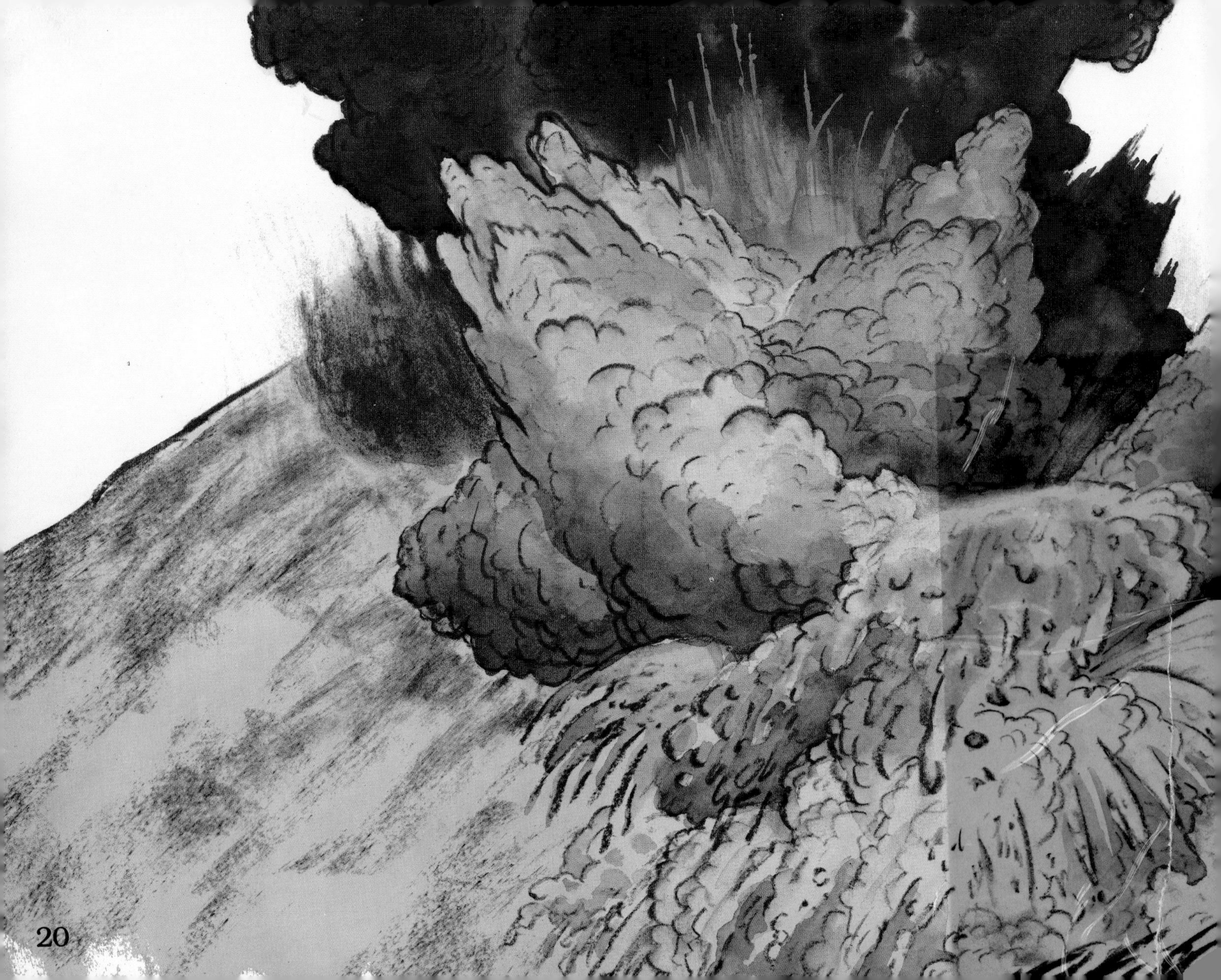

Heat, steam and pressure from the magma blew off the top of the mountain.

Volcanoes don't happen just anywhere.

The map shows where volcanoes are located around the world. You can see that they usually occur where one plate meets another.

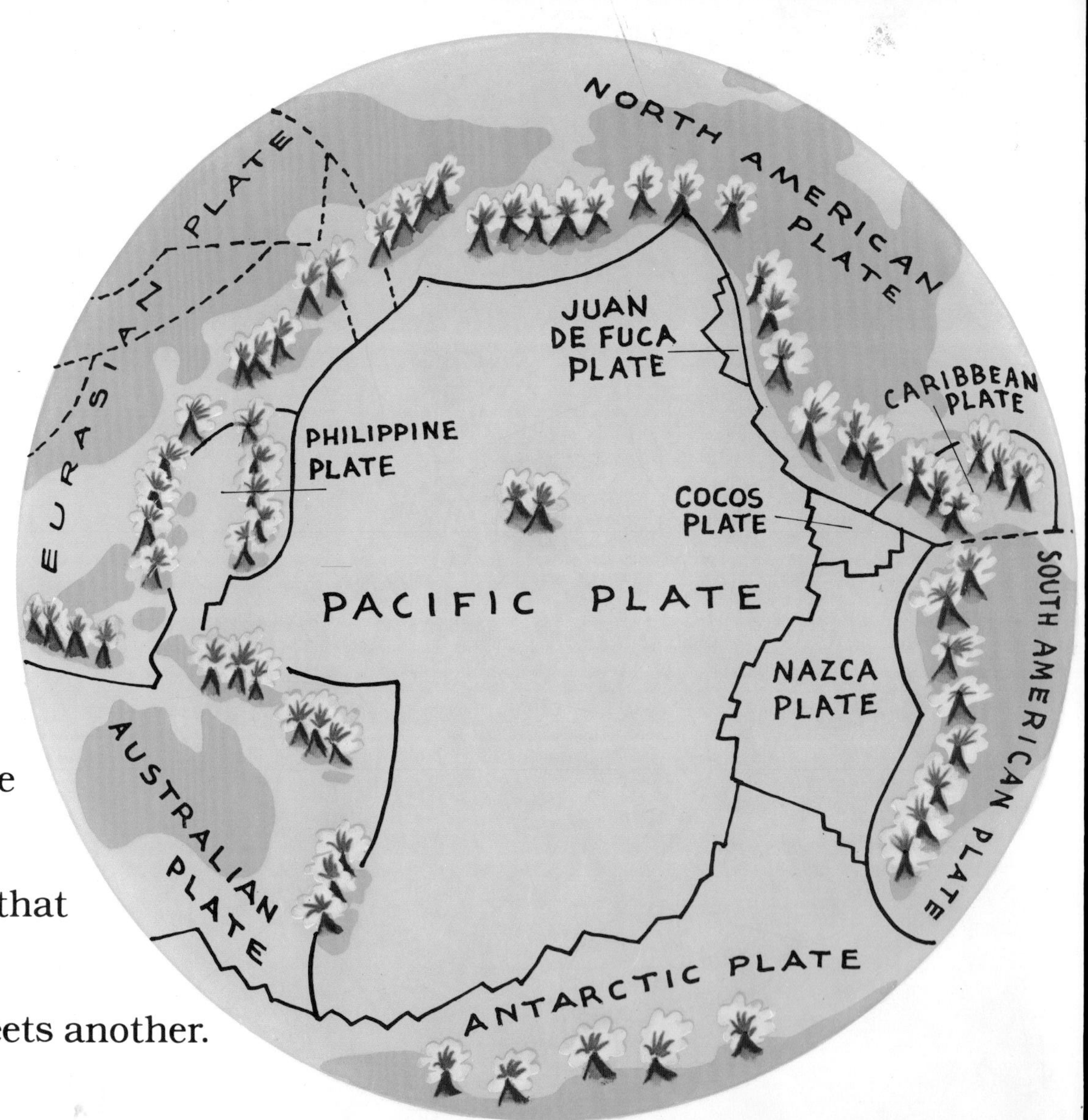

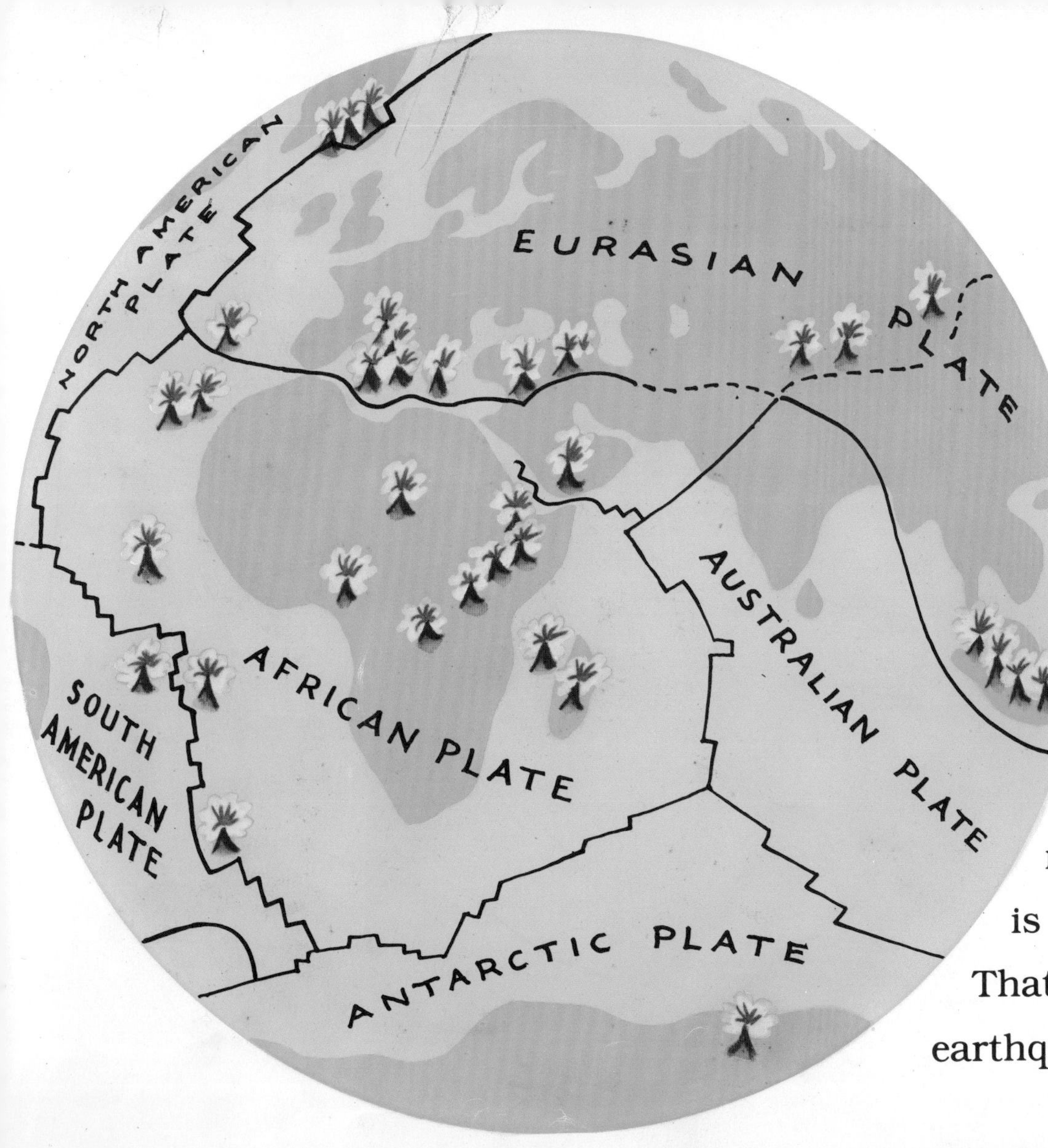

Most volcanoes are along the shores of the Pacific Ocean. They are at the edge of the huge Pacific plate. There are so many that the region is called the Ring of Fire. That's also where most earthquakes occur.

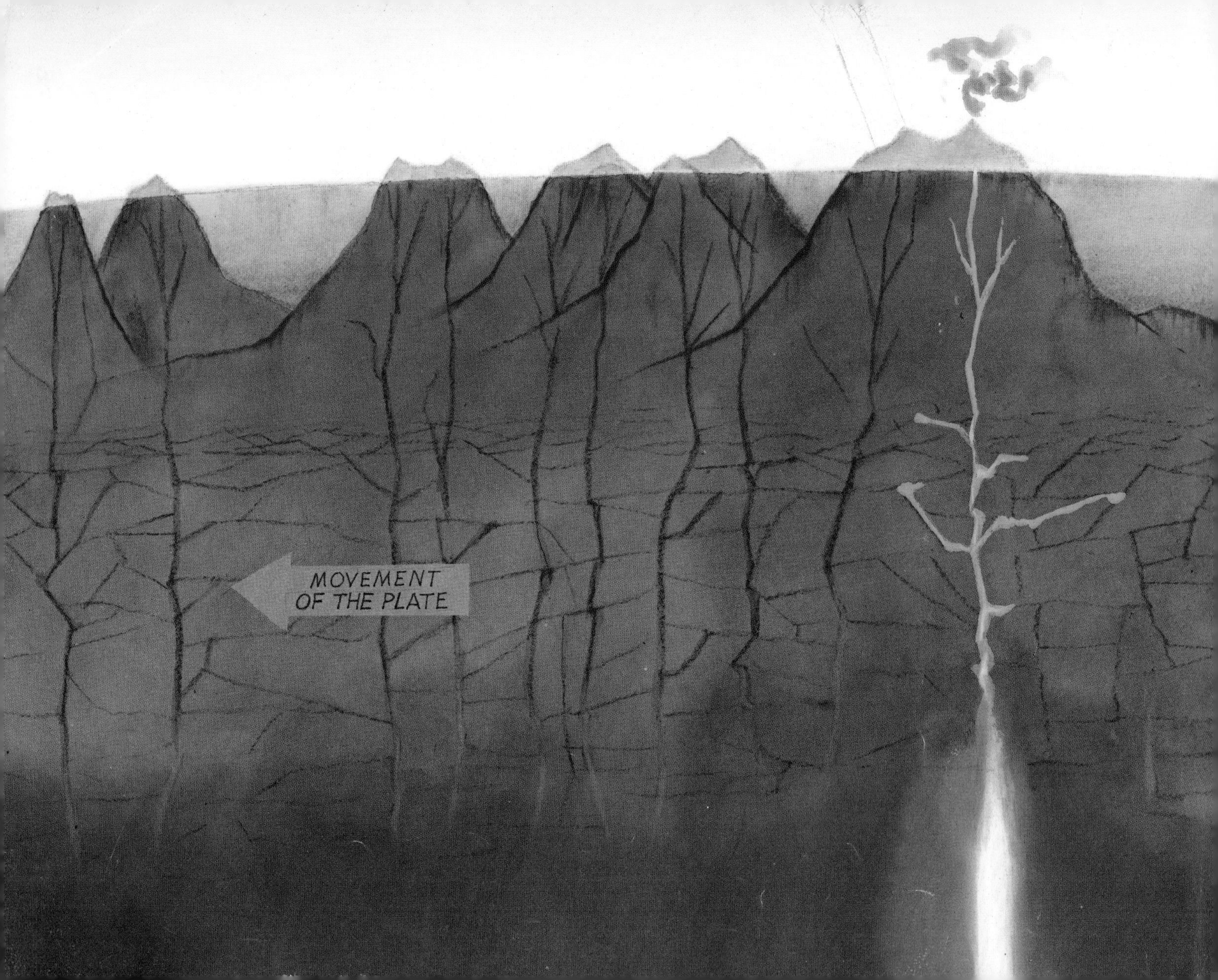
MOVEMENT
OF THE PLATE

Some volcanoes are not on plate edges. Hawaii is in the middle of the Pacific Plate. There molten rock pushes up through a weak spot in the plate. The islands of Hawaii are made from the lava that has built up there.

As the islands have formed, they have been carried slowly northwest by the movement of the plate.

Volcanoes are still erupting on Hawaii. New lava is coming to the surface.

There are thousands of volcanoes around the world. Some erupted millions of years ago, but will probably never erupt again. They are inactive.

Others are active. They could go off again.

From time to time a new volcano will appear.

When a new volcano begins, the ground may get warmer. There may be small earthquakes, and steam may come out of the ground. That's what happened in 1943 at Parícutin in Mexico. Parícutin is on a boundary between two plates. One plate dug under another, and a field became a volcano.

The farmer who owned it, Dionisio Pulido, noticed his field was getting warmer. After a few days the field cracked open, and steam and molten rock spurted out of it. A bulge grew in the field, and it got higher and higher. The field became a hill and then a small mountain. The mountain became hotter and hotter. Rocks, steam, lava and ashes were thrown out of cracks in it.

Ashes covered the countryside. Winds carried them as far as 200 miles away. Houses and churches were covered. Whole towns were buried under ash. Dionisio Pulido's farm was gone. It had become a volcano nearly a quarter mile high.

Geologists cannot tell exactly when a new volcano will be born, or when an old one will erupt. Small earthquakes or rumblings warn geologists that a volcano could erupt tomorrow. Then again, it might be months or even years before it happens.

Geologists do know that most volcanoes will occur along the Ring of Fire. If not there, the volcano will probably occur at the edge of some other plate.

But don't worry about a volcano in your backyard. That doesn't happen very often. Besides, geologists are always watching the earth for changes. Usually they are able to warn us long before a volcano blows its top.